Atomic Theory 7

For Melissa:

In a shared desire for true justice,
In hope for an unyielding faith that,
    even in our utterly flawed state,
    we can help alleviate suffering
    as we approach our work first
                    in love.

                Peace upon you,
                    Trinh

" Love without power is sentimental and anemic.
Power at its best is love implementing the demands of justice.
And justice at its best is power correcting everything
        that stands against love. "

            - Rev. Dr. Martin Luther King Jr.

Atomic Theory 7

poems to my wife and God

by Shann Ray

foreword by Kristin George Bagdanov

with art by Trinh Mai

RESOURCE *Publications* · Eugene, Oregon

ATOMIC THEORY 7
poems to my wife and God

Resource Publications
An Imprint of Wipf and Stock Publishers
199 W. 8th Ave., Suite 3
Eugene, OR 97401

www.wipfandstock.com

PAPERBACK ISBN: 978-1-5326-9584-1
HARDCOVER ISBN: 978-1-5326-9585-8
EBOOK ISBN: 978-1-5326-9586-5

Manufactured in the U.S.A.   JANUARY 2, 2020

for jennifer

To celebrate beauty you must swallow all of death.

—CZESLAW MILOSZ

I want to know how God created this world. To know that what is impenetrable for us really exists and manifests itself as the highest wisdom and the most radiant beauty— . . . There are two ways to live your life. One is as though nothing is a miracle. The other is as though everything is a miracle. God is subtle but not malicious. The most beautiful thing we can experience is the mysterious—it is the source of all true art and science.

—ALBERT EINSTEIN

If one feels the need of something grand, something infinite, something that makes one feel aware of God, one need not go far to find it. There is nothing more truly artistic than to love people. Love is eternal. I always think the best way to know God is to love many things, for therein lies the true strength. Christ is the greatest artist because he does not work in marble and clay and paint . . . he works in living spirit and flesh. He makes living people, immortals.

—VINCENT VAN GOGH

contents

foreword

To the Beloved, Human and Divine

The sun gives life because it is *there* and we are *here*. Any closer, death. Any further, also death. It is the relationship between there and here, that vast, dark distance, that matters. And yet the sun is expanding and that gap is shrinking. And yet, "on earth the sun's light makes hydrogen bombs" (vi.4) and "hydrogen binding bonding is the superstructure at the center of us" (ii.3). The energy of nuclear fusion pulses the sun outward such that scientists say it will consume the Earth in 7.6 billion years, long after you and I and this book are gone. The distance between the atomic and sub-atomic, between sun as life-giving and sun as life-consuming is the distance between the universal and the personal. And yet, every day people die over symbols grown heavy with abstraction and ideologies rusted shut with grief rather than finding in this space "a theology of love," which "is hydrogen binding / in nuclear fusion bonding in our dna" (iii.2). That the same sliver of matter can both make and unmake life depending on a certain slant of light, the position and velocity of bombardment, is the contradiction that energizes this devastating collection of poetry and art.

Shann Ray's *Atomic Theory 7* wrestles with the impossible violence of living. Each line tries to solve the crooked geometry of the "maximum security school to prison pipeline" and balance the unjust equation of "dead millions atlantic american christian slave / trade dead millions north afri-can islamic slave / trade 35 million deaths low estimate the native american holocaust . . ." There is always, it seems, a remainder. A repeating third that stretches into infinity. Ray's method of confronting this paradox is part jeremiad, part ode: he praises and decries the same matter and maker that makes space for such violence. He tries instead to fill this space with love as line after line speeds ahead as incantation, entreaty, apology. No period appears in these poems; they are eternally enjambed. Travelling the length of a day in which whole millennia are contained and configured, this collection follows the sun's arc through the sky, from "Early Dark" to "Night," to trace the impossible alliances and violences of loving and living.

At the heart of Ray's method is steadfastness: to the Beloved both human and divine. A commitment to the face of the other looking back from history and the future. Ray reconfigures the infamous words spoken by J. Robert Oppenheimer at the first nuclear detonation site in Trinity, New Mexico: "I am become death, destroyer of worlds." Considered a mistranslation of the sacred Hindu text *Bhagavad-Gita*, Oppenheimer chooses Death instead of Time as that which destroys all things. Ray offers a reparative reading of this moment, this history: "thermonuclear bombs in abundance o creator o destroyer of worlds" (vi.3). Time, which can be measured by the sun, which we live both inside of and against, is not only that which destroys all things, but creates the conditions of possibility for all life. To live without hope of life is a burden no person can survive.

This reparative work is also enacted by the artwork of Trinh Mai, whose images of collages and paintings throughout the book perform the wounding and the healing that Ray's work articulates, line after line. Mai's work is the needle that joins them, though the gaps between remind us that violence haunts every suture. In *Ba Oi (Dear Father)*, Mai's materials include "living plants, papyrus, rainwater from Việt Nam, copies of Bác Phoủ's release papers from re-education camp, scripture, tears that I shed for him, textile, and palm tree bark on Arches watercolor paper." An altar to injustice and intimacy, she imagines a world in which life grows from bullet holes and wounds are mended by tears. Quoting Cynthia Occelli, Mai reminds us that a seed must be utterly destroyed for life to emerge. That what looks like decomposition might in fact be the composition of a new way of being altogether.

History, it seems, can be read as a series of separations of death and life, light and dark. The intention behind that separation is sometimes holy, but often violent. Haunted by the space between these seemingly incompatible conditions, this collection conjures again and again the light that has the power to both destroy and redeem, revealing the darkness contained within any act of creation, even a poem, a wound stitched open: "o cut us from the cloth sew into us a little death / each death a part of the whole / darkness o never abandon us again" (vi.10). Some day that light will consume everything, yes, but until then, Ray asks the creator / destroyer of worlds:

> o make us
> aware of our infinite
> and atomic obligation
> to each other she and i face to face with you (v.7).

As the poetry editor of *Ruminate Magazine,* I had the privilege of seeing Mai and Ray's work together for the first time in our 47th issue on the theme of "Haunting." It is a rare thing to find two artists whose work complement each other on such a foundational level, and one of the most exciting parts of this project is that the relationship between the poems and art isn't simply ekphrastic—poems written after or in the spirit of the art—but generative, collaborative, and cooperative. Both artists were already creating what they could from the violence of this world and were fortunate enough to find that charge refracted through each other's work. It was a gift to witness this collaboration take root, and this collection is what editors dream will evolve from a chance meeting within their magazine's pages.

Mai writes in the description of her piece, *War Wound:* "As time mends all things, it also reveals the grace that is born out of these moments of grief." And in this reparative, collaborative collection that moves between the violence we continuously inflict on each other and the love we somehow sustain for one another, we learn the possibility of saying something like *We have become Time, mender of worlds.*

—Kristin George Bagdanov

preface
Of Life and Breath

I want to express my deepest gratitude to Trinh Mai for the art that accompanies these poems. Here in these pages her narratives attend her paintings. A true friend and profound artist who embodies the legacy of her family and helps heal the heart of the world, Trinh consistently pursues intercultural dialogue through beauty as a language of peace. Her work is uniquely and prophetically alive, positing the transcendent in communion with the weight of earth and flower, bird and stone, mother and father and child. In her art we find love and sorrow interwoven, and by witnessing our relationship to one another globally in this way, the poems are given life and breath, and the soul is buoyed by courage, resilience, and hope.

Having visited genocide sites in Africa, Asia, Europe, South America, and North America, I have been influenced to change my view of the Divine. Rilke posits a God who is magnificent, and wise, but who is also a God of abandonment. Kenyans, Czechs, Germans, South Africans, Northern Cheyennes, Nez Perce, Blackfeet, Colombians, Canadians, Americans, Japanese, Vietnamese, Chinese and Filipinos—exquisite men and women I've had the honor to know and be known by—have taken me to some of the most ultimate places of human brokenness, compassion, and existence. In that nexus where ultimate violence is committed and somehow also reconciled, I'm struck by the presence of our collective loneliness alongside the gravity of our collective love. At the same time, my wife Jennifer has drawn me into a more contemplative life, and in our shared sense of silence, of listening and action, we began having conversations about space and time, touch, and intentional regard for the dignity of the beloved. In contemplating the Anima Christi (notably the Latin term for the soul of Christ takes the feminine form) we encountered genocide and person to person violence differently, through a lens of atomic theory not at odds with fracture but understanding fracture or fission in the context of fusion. Fusion generates light, and life force, and in a certain sense I think fusion also embodies love. The poems in Atomic Theory 7 accuse us of abandoning one another and abandoning God. In the end, I hope they also help reconcile us with the unforeseen reality of grace.

In using the word 'God' in these poems I'm impressed with how little a person can know of what transcends individual and collective understanding. Doubt wrestles with faith just as solace wrestles with desolation, and I find this interweaving particularly elusive and humbling. Who can know God? Who can deny God? Like love, I find God a mystery not politicized but welcoming, multivalent, embodied in a balance of the feminine and the masculine, surprising, intimate, devastating, and unreservedly beautiful. In the context of the human experience of birth and holocaust, life and breath, exhalation and death, the unity between darkness and light seems to me to be open, composed of untold force, robustly unknowable, and radiant. In this sense, even the most forbidding trauma is not in vain. Love becomes an essential human gift given not only to friends and strangers, but even to one's enemies. Rudolf Otto, in his classic treatise prophetically denouncing fascism in the liminal space between World War I and World War II, referred to God as beyond human discernment. In seeking to gather his thoughts on God he wrote *The Idea of the Holy*, positing the Divine or the numinous as interwoven of three beloved essences he called mysterium tremendum et fascinans. For Otto, as mysterium, the numinous is "wholly other"—entirely different from anything we ordinarily encounter. The numinous evokes a reaction of silence. But the numinous is also mysterium tremendum, provoking terror because it presents itself as overwhelming power. Finally, the numinous is fascinans—merciful, graceful, and imbued with love and peace in the wake of cold fate, in the presence of unavoidable suffering, or in the simple observances of everyday life.

—SHANN RAY

Let us run with patience the race that is set before us, 2019.
Oil on canvas. 60 x 72 inches.

I began this painting shortly after my sister, Kelly, passed in July 2017 after seven long years of battling cancer. She was thirty-seven. Throughout it all, she lived her life with a gentle and vigorous passion that continues to inspire many.

I cradle in my palms a lifeless bird that has finally been released from these enduring wars whose heavy weight is represented by the mighty water buffalo. The rest of us are left here toiling the earth still. Though this may mean having to face further adversity, it also means that we are granted more time to unearth the connections that make for a life fulfilled, like cultivating relationships with our fellow survivors and discovering our place in the world.

After death, life continued, and the painting collected more layers of meaning as it developed over the period of nineteen months, steadily upholding the narrative of freedom. As we've sat with our refugee brethren and sistren and their sons and their daughters to somehow help comfort families during their (our) plight, these gatherings have incited an unceasing prayer for deliverance: *Let our people go.*

> Wherefore seeing we also are compassed about with so great a cloud of witnesses, let us lay aside every weight . . . and let us run with patience the race that is set before us . . .
> —Hebrew 12:1

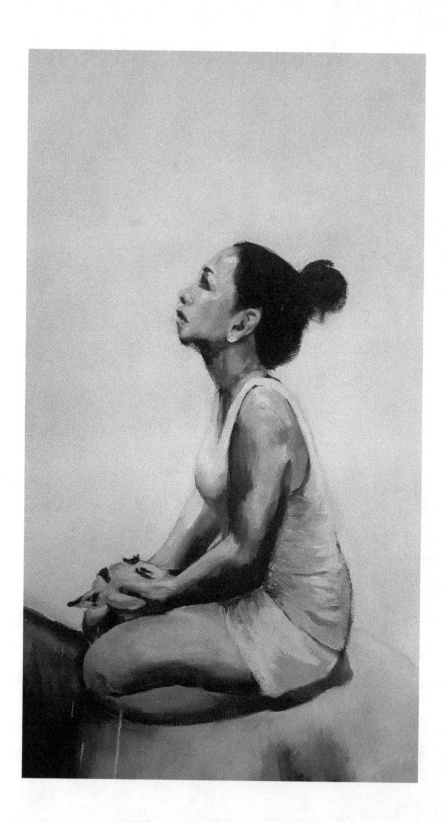

Gathering Light. 2019. Oil on canvas. 47 x 72 inches.

It may be that one of the most burdensome endeavors in life may also present one of the most extraordinary opportunities—to arrive in a place of darkness, and somehow hold the confidence that light dwells somewhere therein. From here, we are granted the capacity to collect the light wherever we may find it, claiming it as our own, and hopefully passing it on to those around us.

As we find ourselves in darkness, our need and yearning for light has a way of expanding our periphery. The light that once may have been positioned out of sight begins passing through the fringes of our broadened vision, and we find ourselves equipped with the ability to see again.

early dark

the body is the city
an elk's ivory bridal teeth
urban wild
nights
wild with beheadings
old guard of the master
order still in effect in our atomic streets
where we wear duct taped shoes to survive the storied ghettos
of liberation the nucleus of the atom the collarbones
of a universe each day stained at the neck

we inhabit the heart of fear but don't believe we end
alone anymore she and i hearing our names
called in the city that is our garment
of praise before dying

i.1

you witnessed you walked
with us among genocidal rape
in rwanda the croat serb siege and when we beheld
hitler stalin mau and infinitesimal quarks the building blocks
of hadrons dead millions atlantic american christian slave
trade dead millions north african islamic slave
trade 35 million deaths low estimate the native american holocaust
much more than 6 million the jewish shoah palestine cambodia the congo
the cheyenne the northern cheyenne with white wounds inside the thighs
on breasts anus genitals
each person you made we love
you we live with you o die with us o know us by name o việt nam the body
of beauty laid down the coeur of love Godspeak the body the alpenglow
in each birdwing is lovely you named each one of us you named us named us

i.2

           bless the harm we do
to the body
o city of God
bless the harrowing fists
we bludgeon each other with

in the living body
the beak of a crow in the shale over hell roaring plateau
is wounding is dissolution of tissue continuity but gently
bless the body o God returning
the hearts of the fathers
to the hearts of their children we need
forgiveness holy Christ we need atonement
the good kiss of our fathers on the cheek
           of our daughters and sons

                                        i.3

the city is black
and brown where men are
chafed strafed shot and my friends
blake walksnice cleveland highwalker
prince jones and k. silk russ
know where love abounds
three dead one still alive receiving

influence bonhoeffer listened
to the church he loved
in harlem and went back
to germany to be hung incinerated
for all his love you'll find his torso still there
in dachau *in cruces* half gold half
burned half buried half risen

i.4

everything held together like water o God
tail fan of a mountain jay
john said life is the light

of women and men sunset ends day ends and here my wife begins
anew her rose and chestnut arms her voice
a troth we keep under stars

she whispers we don't know anything bloodwork is guesswork and hum-
bling
being slain how no one knows or everyone knows none of us knows
even if we are convinced sympathy belongs to you
along with clay and thick descriptions of the world's body

where our doubts fulfill our need horizons shrouded in mist
and our experience of one another as we enfold each other

      is the memory of you
      being glad with us again

                     i.5

you didn't abandon us
we abandoned each other
velocity the separating factor
between bullet penetration and a touch

on the skull we have eyes but don't see
our bodies cityscapes of metal and light
the great loneliness a reminder of how
we die like winter dies
ribcage of a lynx to robe the beloved
you have always loved us in shadow
as porcupines eat femur and fibula
you are there where our nakedness is spar
broom and bonespur you love us her and i
we love you loving our bodies with your many-colored love

i.6

fatherless fathers are the figureheads
of the world wars going on every day
the master recursively conceiving slaves
swollen by violence in the national park
above jackson hole the tine of a moose antler
through the eye of one who wanted photos

the body absorbs natural forces
except forces which cross the limits
of elasticity or resistance
bruised pierced john jesus johannes josef maria
mother jones came crying out
from the wilderness prepare
the military industrial prison complex
prepare the wind of God blow wind blow

i.7

even in darkness o God
I witness your pleasure the light
of morning not yet on her face
her orbital bones of loosestrife and flume
our faces touched by you and gladness
more physical than we know
less temporal more present
more contained in the breath
we breathe
we only live only breathe
each day her unbraided hair down over me
the lace at the window
embroidering us silver
in the dark still sleeping before dawn

i.8

she and i love you
o Lord our strength
fire from your mouth
consumes us coals kindled
in your mouth our dark skin
where you parted the veil at the door
of our room saying white calls dark
dark and white white the hangman's rope
o move us through the house off the front
stoop thick darkness under your feet
outside to where you ride
angels down soar on winds' wings
make darkness your covering abundant
lightning the canopy around you the rain

i.9

out of the black body
of your presence
come clouds
and lightning
you speak thunder
heavenly sound
and return walking
light on your feet
entering the house again
to recline with us
and we say o meadlowlark sing
and bitterroot bloom light our lamp
humble my enemy my enemy me
fine as windblown dust

i.10

knowable center of all things all the world
is below you and you are all
around and inside her with love
for her with love for him with love
for them us women men
and we are singing rivers widening
at the mouth strings of subatomic life
vibrating into the sea infinity loop harmonics
of all our relative and quantum loves
wild raking of wind like worship
she and i wandering back to each other grateful
for your quiet voice in our home open-roofed
on nights where we lie on our backs
and you hold the stars in place

i.11

coming in the likeness of

the blood; and

these women

if one member suffers, all
suffer with *it*; or if

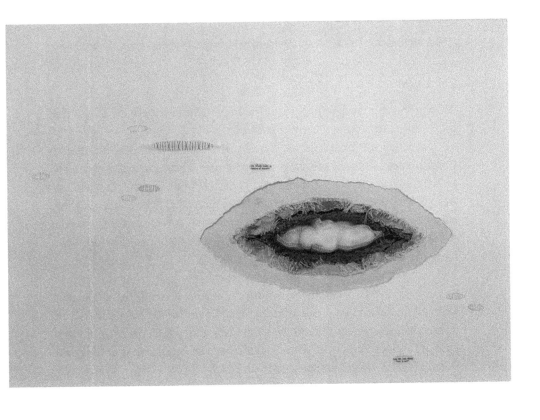

If One Member Suffers, 2019. From the *Mẹ Ơi (Dear Mother)* collection. Scripture, thread, and tree bark on paper. 6 ½ x 6 1/2 inches.

War Wound, 2017. Bà Ngoại's (Grandmother's) thread, cotton, paper, scripture, and textile. 18 x 25 ½ inches.

Among the commonalities that we the living all share, perhaps one of the most profound is our collective need to heal.

The delicate materials used to craft these physical and emotional wounds speak on their sensitive, tender nature. These lacerations have afflicted us with discomfort, pain, and heartache, but like salt on an open wound, the sting somehow aids in our healing. And although this suffering is hardly welcomed, it has the potential of serving as a catalyst for a period of transformation and revival, igniting a strength within us that we might have not known existed otherwise.

As time mends all things, it also reveals the grace that is born out of these moments of grief, the invaluable lessons learned, the significant Truths that surface, and the kindling of a Compassion that pierces even deeper than the wounds themselves. And when they heal, they stamp upon us these unique scars as proof of the intrinsic strength that has, time and time again, led to our conquest over adversity.

has the sun risen
than it wis

before dawn

century man teeth haggard or precise
fatherless when you slap my face
i know narcissistic rage is just a reaction
to narcissistic injury the master egos march
                    our dna our cells made of light two parts
hydrogen conducting light one part oxygen
hydrogen makes bonding energy in our dna 10 billion antigens
created through binding energy for a given
immunity response the breath of life
                    even after smothering abrasions around the mouth and
        nose
make us respond defensively becoming breathing bombs
swords death-pikes flames detaching emotionally
to escape more injury any harm real or imagined to our fantastic magical
thinking
and again we solicit narcissistic supply subservience adulation admiration
being feared

                                    ii.1

o hold us in your arms wing us not afraid
of education and self-respect you who are our home always

fathers rape sons rape daughters we are loathed in bogalusa louisiana
you are love we are lonely cotton belt deep south lonely
we beat our children on the face or body
where abrasions indicate a struggle
wives husbands mothers fathers
blood whip one another strike each other's skulls
with bricks bottles burn holes in each other
gash knife wounds in the flesh abandon and butcher each other
hide the bodies in broad daylight under leaves or light dirt
murder mother father child blood love we invent you God
o corollary to our illusions but you won't be
invented you who love harmony simply are

ii.2

                                                      and so she believes

love a natural state
created by you God so she asks me to value wailing women
for they teach our daughters to wail and remember america
slaves raped collared killed and why we are responsible
for each other and how we depend on each bloodacre housed in the soul
and i say now we have valid reliable measures of forgiveness capacity and
soon
atonement capacity and since we can measure biophotons knitted inside
the body
and how the eyes don't grow old and can contain more concentrated light
each day
atomic particles waves of light are called quanta then we also know dna
hydrogen binding bonding is the superstructure at the center of us a
subatomic nuclear architecture she says she knows it helps us believe the
deeper the light in her body
marked moled the more contained the higher our forgiveness capacity one
to one
she and i agreeing over dinner and this night horse constellation science
discovers it too
because art is science is beauty is us knowing how fear torments and love
heals

                              ii.3

                              31

once i thought you were loneliness
because that's what i was told
and that's how i felt but now i believe
your name is love because i find love the banked fire
                              of rooms where your body is not es-
                    trangement but desire
still so many of us so harmed makes longing a knife wound
Christ how my wife kisses me when I'm unmade by pain
my daughters hold me do we really know

your name she and i always wondering
when in mortal dread we remember the insect-whitened
skull of a mule deer below the forked tine pattern

I'm afraid Jesus but with your kiss on my cheekbone
and upward on my temple the agony is something
radiant dark radiance please keep me alive for now for them

                                        ii.4

on the mountain each child a sparrow
attended by ghostpipe and yellowjackets
each woman cherished by her children each father beloved
nagasaki hiroshima new york city everywhere burning occurs
along the 10th parallel the christo-islam nightdays war of nigeria the sudan
somalia indonesia malaysia the philippines at ground zero o land water oil
love
o windbird she said o wounds of God command us not to be afraid
remember we are the least of these
for everywhere the mature atheist believer understands kindness
while the hard believer atheist has contempt and below
contempt cruelty each dead but alive for beauty is wellbeing
crux cruces coeur corpus the soul o Anima Christi
with plain old parricide infanticide in our pockets
o death hang and body kiss

ii.5

33

                                        we want to ask your forgive-
ness will you forgive us
as we lie on the floor in the house
disrupting the supremacy our bodies in the form of a cross her body over
mine
mirroring mine my breathing echoing her breathing over me
spherical energies at the heart of matter range
the surface of the world forgiveness first before atonement
because we believe what martin and corretta said
in america the oppressor will never willingly give up power
yet by loving the oppressor we bring about not only our own salvation
but the salvation of the oppressor listen she says for a loving
message from God transparent we transmit light or we don't
what does God say what do you say we whisper
we are pulverized fused harmonized from the silence your voice
in our bodies rein bittercress stonecrop toadflax mountain-heather

                              ii.6

in the capital city where the unfamiliar name
is love God is water mountain bluebird and daffodil
ladyslipper devil's club and penstemmon
your mercy for all women and men your beloved breath for all clay
where physics and metaphysics kiss o lift our faces breathe into our
mouths

you were never meant to be abandoned God
jim mcpherson proposed each world citizen approximate
the ideals of the world be on conversant terms with it
carry each culture inside for by wearing these clothes like a V of shed
horns
we are a synthesis mercy the responsibility uniting quantum mechanics
and relativity
God we abandoned you but let us die generously our hands upturned
like votive candles the spirit comes fractures the air with iridescent fire
with terror
with indelible gladness written on our skin the garment we shy from
before we open
like hungry nuclear children and eat please split atoms in us she and i
starving to death

ii.7

beaten taken
to the trucks to be gassed
to the ovens to be made
ash in such proficient chambers
what is to give light must endure burning
first stabbed then forcibly drowned first directed to dig
our own graves before execution
head chest chest bullet holes we murder
you God more each day our bodies hung from trees bridges
overpasses in the bright cities glittering bruises an effusion
of blood on the earth due to rupture the sloughing
of flesh from bone-dead eyes bloated by sun
ogled by zealots and masses or seen by none
i said the soul of God is feminine but she said it's both

ii.8

where bear claws ring the bear white skull put your hand
gun in the offering plate poet ethanol products
get transported through kansas from los angeles to new york
the family lives in cardboard anything helps the city the body
even when it hurts taya smith said i'll sing until
the miracle comes a synthesis sweet brown
black white city country provincial universal alive
with these contradictions again jim mcpherson intimated
we have earned the right to call ourselves citizens of the world
and heaven she adds jim's and yours God she and i and you
a grown man sobbing in our arms bruised by blunt force
by fist stone stick whip boot who forgives like you
the mountains above glacier gunsight and wolf
and the sigh from my beloved's chest after

ii.9

those better than me are dead so why am i alive
as you light each morning and gild the swallow's back

because of her i try to believe you are not alone we are with you

she gives you the water you ask so kindly for the song
she asks me to sing you give us your hand on her heart
no surface between us skin to skin
in accord with the elemental properties of light fusion is union
with the beloved in love in silence in joy
the stars bring word
of your grace in the darkness your body a hammer

you live in our house
like flood dawn
but still i study so much the arts of unbelief
o windburn and dustwork thirsty on my tongue

                                    ii.10

she and i often say how glad we are
we have so many sisters and brothers
their faces like unveiled stars
their engines sacred in flame
so when we drive to the edge of the cliffs
above the beartooth plateau we know the sun
is our own and you the web of light below

these trees of spectral color silvered by the constellations

the ground beneath us is dark
and your burden light
the meadowlark the swift the swallowtail
our feet are dimly illumined and hope still continuous
o sister windbird brother fire is there anything more
beautiful than a woman leading the people in praise

ii.11

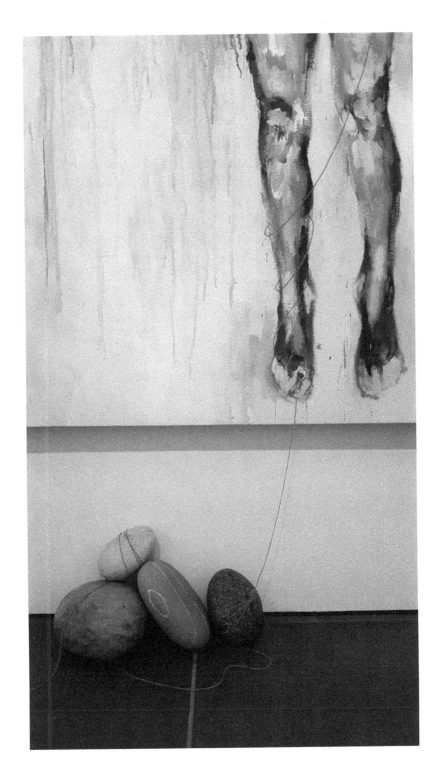

Reaching for Things Unseen, 2016. Hand embroidery and oil on canvas, thread, and stones gathered from Pacific shores. 49 x 72 inches.

When we think about the things that are the most invaluable to the human spirit, we might find that the things we seek are often those things unseen—the boundless strength that awakens when we recognize that it resides within, the uplifting comfort that we find in a hope for something that is yet to come, and the faith that holds us firmly as the rubble trembles below our feet.

Here, a woman reaches for the virtues that fortify her, helping to loosen the burden that strives to dishearten her by its mighty weight.

sunrise

these fatherless fathers
are the fathers of loneliness

annihilation born of them and their lovelessness
men with gone eyes abrasions contusions lacerations
incised wounds stab wounds wounds by firearm in towns in lidice

in sand creek in fort robinson in stellar nucleosynthesis
the natural abundances of the chemical elements within stars
change some men exist with no light
in their eyes
nuclear fusion reactions in the cores and overlying mantels of stars
these men were abandoned
their hands harm us their fractures and dislocations
we are anyway the dogwood blossoming bloodmark on our forehead
hands and feet our side your kisses

iii.1

here in the still point
where the wind doesn't blow
the wing of a blackbird
at the corner of her mouth
a flock follows
curtaining the sky

a theology of love is hydrogen binding
in nuclear fusion bonding in our dna
and still all our fatherlessness
mass graves suicides killings
loathings which are not
your thoughts but ours
our hard dark engine
our birdless days

iii.2

we have tongues
but don't taste

the blood of a boar who has eaten
his young

she and i did not hear until we heard
singing a whispering of the steller's wings
in our sleep

waking us through all the starry abundances
windbone she is in love
inside you and wombing she is acquainted
with fusion nucleons forming a helium nucleus
in the interior of stars never mind how

a bullet that pierces the jaw and ricochets
off the shoulder blade becomes lodged in the lung

iii.3

on the third day
before the nuclei of hydrogen-specific light elements
forced together under extremely high pressure fuse
into heavier nuclei and release enormous energy
after we proceed to eat our young
we should wonder at ourselves but we're so hungry we ignore it

o sentimental Christ kissing mother marry the military father
o apathetic stone father marry the rage child-mother the deadish one
at dawn on the first day when the devil is more real than we imagined

o liver of my brother procreate cruelty
o finger of a child birth-strangled
by the umbilical cord o braying ass and bandy witch
one single terrible damnation

betrayed by lack of beauty imprisoned by the state emptied ashen lit

iii.4

we abandoned our children in northern europe
in order to advance our own lives but it backfired due to
corrosive acids alkalis injuries simple grievous
or electricity radioactivity gasses and hyperbolic force

abandonment is not of you

God wombing is o intimate wombing
the silvertip grizzly just below the rocky mountain front
wandering the fens in his 900 pound body the circumference
of his neck four feet around o God
before i met my wife I knew abandonment
for what it was suicide max born said we can't control knowledge
there are absolute limits obscuring knowledge
the abandonment where physical and metaphysical
meet entombing our children for generations

iii.5

the planets exist
wombing us in you my wife says
for you remember when we were born
and you remember us from before

like satellites coursing through space unfamiliar
with time we were born to venture each other
your love o God a passion
in which you create poems women and men
sainfoin prince pine wax currant
intricate incomplete fathers and mothers
in love and lovers brookfoam and willowherb
like big animals who don't eat one another's children
so lovely unabused and not abusive they won't
abandon us

iii.6

at sunrise made of night the two one light
we find or rather feel self-laceration is not of you
nor mechanical injuries nor blunt force
sharp force firearms not you nor self-worship
for what is you contains nuclear star fields
without abrasion smooth as the neck of a dove
the ember of the long kiss your lips breathing
life into us like fire she and i locked to each other
and unlocking for contempt is bloody
and light makes blood more visible
when i see my brother's body headless in the dirt
i am only a small flare of light under the door
between this world and
before the light goes out

iii.7

the stars are not lonely they have each other she says
ante-mortem abrasions reddish brown slightly raised in vital reaction
post-mortem abrasions yellow translucent star-forming nebulae
over bony prominences the earth the rainflower
mountain lions sunning on benches of stone atop the great divide
her hands teach me not to miss bone and use primary flight feathers
instead

we are already home because the sun is fusion

she brought me close and read to me again yesterday how john said you
are light
and Christ said i am the light of the world come to me
and you will have no darkness you will have the light of life the open
wheat field
of forgiveness is wishbone is love is light splitting matter with light
a boon to the body corretta martin the wings of western tanagers
singing love without power is windless anemic weak
and power without love is reckless o fusion wind carry us forever now

iii.8

we have a mother made of well-being a father full of love fully loving
and below them is you who are the God of love who made them

she has convinced me even if fission bombs of uranium plutonium tho-
rium
are bombarded with light so critical mass erupts in chain reactions
chains of fission events weighing up and vaporizing matter
into grey-lilac clouds of ungodded shape at once natural unnatural
o flip the deathswitch external signs of serious internal injury
suicidal and homicidal abrasions differentiated
from erosion of skin produced by ants excoriation by excreta
pressure sores out of them came children
she and i thankful beautiful pasqueflower fleabane
elephanthead vervain created by love to be in love

were we to love fully
we were

iii.9

i've used a bone saw to remove
the skull plate of a whitetail buck
the crown a five by six in opposition and alignment
not unlike apathetic brooding rodlike bipolar fathers
or frenetic bipolar mothers who clutch claw
to keep from falling

manner of injury known by distribution
in throttling curved abrasions made by fingernails on the neck
they walk through my door staring dead-eyed
into the next world

their splintered faces splitting the nuclei producing collisions
igniting the suicide engine with unknown binding energy
traces detected environmentally worldwide we blame them yes us
even as the doe descends the mountain in the evening to drink

iii.10

o God creating
woman and man in the image of God
you created them she sings from our small room in the predawn dark
the major axes of light-bearing electrons revolve
elliptic on the form of a rosette around the nucleus

convincing me here at least for a moment she and i know each other
our hands know our children are love and loved they change us
and we receive them owl-clover deer-vetch and currant with gratitude

seeing you in them she also imagines angels on the electromagnetic spec-
trum
she leans her body into mine in our bed saying they go undetected it's all
just light
too powerful to be seen and you infinitely more so

with our daughters asleep in our arms we remember we are windbone
exiles haunted by our past and barefoot we whisper to them do you feel
deeply loved
and yes they open their eyes the iris starlike wondrous yes

iii.11

When We Became Trees, 2014. Acrylic, charcoal, gouache, hand embroidery, and ink on paper. 56 x 40 inches, diptych.

I am ever inspired by the wisdom of nature and the way she grows, heals, and embraces her own time. The collective rhythm shifts, the seasons pull, and the migrations come. And then they go. As the Pacific expands and exhales at her own cadence, the tides rise and subside, and all that is born of her belly breathe easy for they appreciate that out of this rhythm comes new growth and new life. The trees, too, know that they are on time for their lives. They release their blossoms to cultivate space for new growth, and they rest for a time to gather the necessary strength for an abundant, fruitful season that lies ahead. Their habit is always to reach for light because they understand that it is only in this light that they will continue thriving.

Husband and wife find stillness in a garden of native southern California plants, all of which can be used as medicine to promote healing. As a canopy of eucalyptus shelters them, yerba santa, yerba mansa, poppies, and dandelions cushion every step on their path. Flickers assist the couple in adopting nature's perfect rhythm. Like the trees, man and woman stand confidently upright and on solid ground. And like the trees, they trust in their own time.

midday

she kisses me
holds my face in her hands

says our duty is to love
with all of our being focused on the beloved
einstein's "very interesting conclusion"
coupling time and space
in prayer our bodies a single destiny
or rather entity
we were never
meant to be lonely
we were meant to be

fully known a stem of timothy
in the city a conundrum
of prayer

iv.1

my wife wants us to know
everything
of each other's darkness
a nuclear even incendiary
arrangement solemn and just
between us fecked bobtail and nightshade
the transfer of force through the body
results in wounding power
we've had no affairs
we're not lucky or bragging
we're just remembering
the atomic look in our friend's
eyes when the lights went out
and only smoke remained

iv.2

we are alive as 55 million of us die
each year 150,000 each day we are alive
bullet holes in the face neck and chest
like small ink wells we are alive with you
we inhale life and exhale death so when i say i love you i die
and when you say you love me i live with you
over all in and outside us your generous voice singing to us arise
God you are not afraid to die
the earth and sky will fall
but after all terror subsides
after the knife-worked throat
a dark necklace above the clavicle
love remains love we are stunned by
the city she and i keeping our feet from nature from knowing

iv.3

she places her body in the nook of mine
saying God is never gone

not silent distant cold or dead not what we make God
God is and has never not been
passed through death bringing death through us God

brought death to the subatomic nucleus
of ultimate theory revealing ultimate forgiveness
a fusion field hovering in the heart of matter

beargrass plumes on the ascent of going to the sun road

for dogmatism is what we call mechanical injury
caused by physical violence but anything is far less
knowable than we know especially God so break us
she says break us into being as you break open
the fields of flowers on the mountain

iv.4

we hear them every day women and men
sent by you God
gritty how you speak our names our days
even as you breathe the stars and pronounce
their number o when will we stop slashing
our wrists and hanging ourselves
saint augustine said praying means closing your eyes
and knowing God is creating the world even now
you know what lies in the darkness and where
light dwells o God believe in her and speak
trees and animals cowslip and spurge the bear ursus arctos horribillis a
river of swans
for we are one we are rain you are river o make us responsible
for each other for how we turn
our faces and where we lie down to sleep

iv.5

you are formless
a bear's paw four times the size of a man's hand
she says and when we think of you again
we refuse to see fate as anything
but a convention constructed by privilege
disabused of power so open outward she says

do not foreclose on doubt or reify faith

our calcified theological atheist minds are less beautiful
than our modest ones the perforating bullet passes through and is
less damaging than a wounding object lodged inside us
i like gravity through which worlds pass
a brood of common copper
butterflies among bunch grass and blue willow
and you like water through bear trap canyon

iv.6

we need you she says
you want us to be
a nautilus of intimacy

the knot of her ankles and wrists

harnessing the power of atoms
even if it's true due to distribution of force a knife causes more damage
than a blunt weapon but less than a fireball's blast winds

such force driven with such disequilibrium is not you God but white
misogynist God and misandry contempt for men God
not God but our conception of God for God is the loveliest form she
gestures
to the spanish colombian woman kissing the black feet of Christ
in the alcove of la sagrada familia her hand in mine my hand in hers
nothing more needed she sighs as you sigh
you are all women old and young all men

iv.7

71

the smell of smoke from the trees in autumn
how creative the scent of auburn
crushed beneath our feet and how
we create moments of light and flash blindness through
thermonuclear pulse energy heat of suns winds of hurricanes
from weapons emitting large amounts of light and heat
and we too absorb and emit light and heat
returning to annihilation against our better judgment

for force subjects body tissue bone and organ
to shear and compression traction mechanical insult
fission the division of one into two
fusion the union of two becoming one
the character of light's velocity unchanging so we find you
in red and gold from the beginning to now falling through our arms to the
ground

iv.8

in this world where license owns the city
she is still modest and so she is free
not only art for her model but her eyes on the infinite
wounds we bear wounds born in subatomic bodies split
or better fused to harness more light
no longer against love for love
for when you who are fire put your hand out to her
she touches you and though you are fire you are also
the body she holds close and the bear she witnesses
jaw hinge of the silvertip with claws four inches in length
to facilitate climbing digging for food dismembering carrion

or eating white chalk moths by the bushel go tell your beloved God says to
my beloved
what he wants to know of nutrients and everything night windswept cold
but tell him also of fire

iv.9

73

world without
end amen
a bison's shoulders are so big because the head weighs 300 pounds
similarly God in the lion's shoulder and the lamb's chest the dawn
the dusk movement of the body in the direction of force
is less wounding than movement contrary to force
every night she and i love
with happiness insistence and the infinity required to cross the light bar-
rier
the deep longing transparent in the curvature of space
for gravity unites us wings us even as the exact composition of light
eludes physicists similar to the way the lift of her eyebrow the recesses
of her jaw and neckline her collarbones elude description like elkbone
breastplates
or an elktooth dress o God i see now nothing travels faster
than light except perhaps grace the distance between stars

                                        iv.10

everything has always existed
and before it God knew us she says
can you imagine
you and i always
enough for God and love and the fusion that powers every
subatomic sequence and also high magnitude stars

things don't exist because of us bobcat paw or hereford jowl
we exist in loving the things of this world
God and angelic creatures wolfsbane
devil's club penstemon
wolverines working
with great speed above the tree line
and suicides guardians of the soul o wounds of God

iv.11

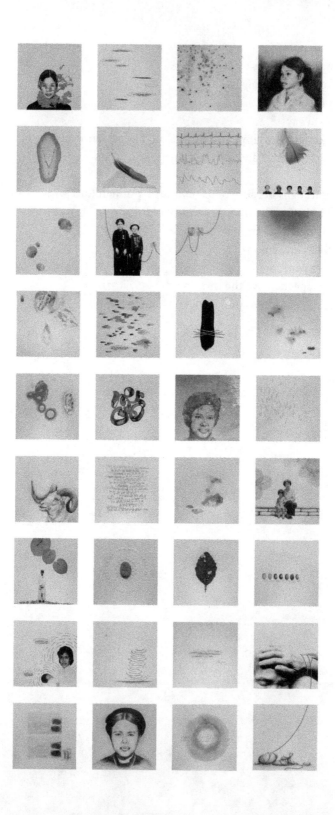

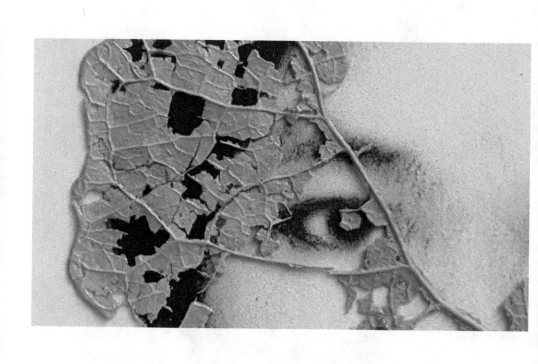

Mẹ Ơi (Dear Mother), 2019. Acrylic, my blood and hair, Bà Ngoại's (Grandmother's) ashes and hair, charcoal, color pencil, egg shells, fractured wishbone, fragment of Bà Ngoại's unread letter, feathers from Mẹ's rooster, family photos, fish bones saved from a family dinner, graphite, Chị Tư's gold leaf, hand embroidery, imprints from flora and soil from Bà Ngoại's garden, ink, plant material, rice, scripture, stone, tattered feather, Vietnamese newspaper, stamp received from Việt Nam, and wax dripped from candle burned for my maternal lineage on paper and vellum. 6 ½ x 6 ½ inches.

In the winter of 2014, we gathered around Bà Ngoại during her last days of life to patiently usher her into the next. A heart-rending moment arose when Mẹ placed her hand upon Bà Ngoại's forehead, both furrowed with the lines that told the story of an interwoven life that met toil with strength and weariness with faith. She mournfully called out to her mother, *Mẹ ơi*.

These words seared themselves upon the flesh of my inner chambers, and they continue to haunt me still. I absorbed Mẹ's wavering voice as I sat at Bà Ngoại's feet, arrested by the lengthening tone of each echoing call.

Mẹ ơi.

Mẹ ơi.

As I witnessed this intimate moment between mother and mother, daughter and daughter, I ruminated on the expansive love that they held for one another—this deep love that rendered them the might to carry such overbearing weight for one another—the nine months that sustained a hope to bring life and light into our lamenting world, and the boundless sacrifices that followed thereafter. I thought about how the roles can shift as we children shoulder the burdens for our mothers out of this same inherited sense of devotion—this promise of a love that does not boast as sacrifices made remain unseen and unheard.

This piece is part of a collection of thirty-six works that hearken unto the Mother. Portraits from five generations of mothers and daughters within my family comprise this body that speaks on the burden that mothers carry for their children, and the afflictions that their children, in turn, carry for them.

dusk

in late light i saw
a blue heron standing in the shallows of pine creek

it's not hard to see you
moving the bodies of the sky
or walking in plain clothing to where we sleep

you kiss our eyelids
and the skin below our wrists
where the gashes are
for out of the deep we call unto you so many of us the rope at our neck the
knife
the gun pressed to our temple where stars approximate blackbody radi-
ance
the heat of the blackbody increasing the sum of light emitted per second
she and I have loved this heat these stars and through them you sent forth
to everyone o give us the will
to die for enemies and strangers and friends

V.1

we don't need to act like we don't see you
we see the light in her hair the sky so bloodmade

the evening an oblong bruise
the century just began and with it more killings and greater
tenderness these two divide showing the medallion flare
of aspen leaves the coat we wear in the new fall not unlike the old silence
dread and awe of negative theology of the humiliated Christ
infinitely more than the material positivism so fatal to science

like science when calcified all fixed system theologies are too ugly
too certain and counter to God beauty the wind
the sickle is the sower when critical mass and chain reaction
result in a fireball five miles in diameter over russia
the first thermonuclear pulse loosens the joints the second
obliterates all vaporizes matter the city the body

V.2

she and i are too intimate
and not intimate enough
we think of this too as a bruise
the way a blow by rod or stick produces two parallel linear hemorrhages
and the verdict: God said light has come into the world
but men loved darkness more than light

because their deeds were evil the intimacy of wickedness
is not intimacy but abandonment
enlarged and irregular

and still we think of this as an eagle thinks of her wings
over the great divide her delight in the long flight the dakota 38

plus 2 and wounded knee creek the body meant for great things her eyes
the horizon
where sun breaks the world and warms her back
turning her flight feathers gold

v.3

my wife whispers to me just before sleep
saying holiness is her son the one we
miscarried the two
we miscarried and i don't disagree

the spoon of her hips ushered the dead

holiness is her daughter
too i believe our daughters are holy
thank you for speaking to me directly

through them i still hear your voice
on their lips o God saying I love you saying
the most powerful things are also the most
irreducible just as music makes the broken whole
your hands are their hands unafraid
when i'm old to touch my face

v.4

sorrow of the great sorrow
by the acts of colonialism and imperialism
we put the category of human under the severest pressure
and below the great sorrow
we encounter despair and further below gladness

if you comprehend God it's not God she says
with augustine o God help her and me
see through your eyes you are often drawing us
close saying something quietly
profound the blessed uncertainty being we don't know what being means

we hear you saying to us you are meant to bear
each other's sorrow the beloved community even caught in the curved
jaws
and steel foot plate of the human trap your love is footfall over the earth
marked by men
like sunlight bears life o bear us darkly on

v.5

I was born in the city of industry
but my window looked out on four mountain ranges

mornings women and men walked the earth
oil and dust on their feet
and men gave women a lock of their hair and women gave men
the sun seven times brighter

wing me to where
you want me

i was raised on scientific understanding but found a light in her
like the light of seven days and found science one with you God
for when you bind the bruises of all people and heal our wounds
the dust is not dust the eyes conduct light from us to others
our bodies made of dawn but sightless and at last when we go to bed
she and i hold hands like young lovers

v.6

o make us
aware of our infinite
and atomic obligation
to each other she and i face to face with you
remind us to kiss you with the kisses of our mouth
she asks me to be more devoted to her than to myself
more devoted to us than to her more devoted to you than us

police shootings chokings fingernails dig and thumb arches collapse the
windpipe
making me aware of the worlds circling
the blood of the sow who has eaten her young and the cities we live in
american male white male dark white break us God
kiss us until we breathe with atomic breath the substantial
air of atonement our beautiful lips not ours but yours
their beautiful face your face

v.7

we too like schwarzchild's dark stars
frozen celestial ravenous
body marks from straps belts chairs chains
make a darker imprint blows from whips
are elongated o help us know
each of us being the vault of the Divine
we are often unlucky disenfranchised
struggling to pay the bills make the rent hold on our hold
slipping from our fingers as we frantically move our feet
to keep from drowning o help us know this is not uncommon
but simply what it means when we bombard the nucleus
of the adam for two to become one
solace safe haven harbor the eve
the evening star good hesperus and the applewine of your kiss

v.8

she and i walked with you God and into your kitchen
it was not a gleaming tower but a place warm with laughter
and delicious food

energy is the body times the velocity of light squared
for subatomic theory
is resurrection theory

we didn't circle high and far from you God
because you were not far
you were near and we heard you singing
and touched the fine wrinkles
around your eyes smiling
as you spoke to us saying
we are the wildest storms and the songs you sing

the firethorn the falcon o God flourish on the mountain

v.9

when I was a boy our hunting dog ran through the woods to lay at our feet
tiny spears the color of wild things had pierced the wall of her cheek
she whimpered as my father plied the porcupine quills from her mouth

we are a landscape on the back of our hands
a flock of starlings a dark light rising
from a small tree light is energy sent through time and space
at a velocity of 671 million miles an hour

light circles the earth seven times in one second
travels from the sun to our skin in eight minutes
crosses the milky way in 100,000 years
emanates from the andromeda galaxy to us
in 2.5 million years and from us
to the edge of the observable universe in 46.5 billion years

the universe is still expanding and we are minute solitaries but in love

V.10

two things dostoyevsky said:
beauty will save the world
and nothing is more beautiful than Christ

tell us of your stark trees Christ standing cold
place our hands into the coarse black coat of winter wolves

we cannot un-name you God three swallowtail skulls in my hand
what does Christ even mean
she and i cannot un-remember you

one goiter a necklace of two dead hummingbirds

tell me of your sky a red field behind trees
and how you drink water through rock

Lord of wonder Lord of night
where dark smudges the world rim
blast us with wind and light

V.11

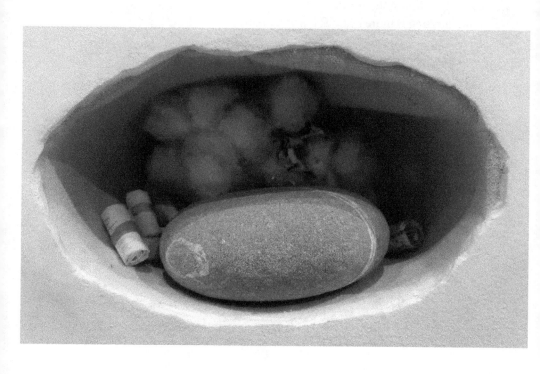

That We Should Be Heirs, 2019. Bà Ngoại's (Grandmother's) letters that I promised would remain unread, cotton plucked from the farm from which my husband's family once harvested when they first arrived in America, hand embroidery, holy water, stones collected from the Pacific Coast, raw canvas, personal hand-written scrolls contributed by community members, thread, Pacific Ocean water, and wool.

There is a Vietnamese belief that we must give our dead a proper burial so that their souls can rest. This installation invites us to bury our fears and our burdens so that we might find a moment of rest before marching forth.

In my recent work, stone has represented the weight that we have carried for ourselves and for those whom we love. For millions and billions of years, these stones have endured tremendous pressures. They have been thrust against hard surfaces, tumbled over rough edges, broken down by violent falls, all to become exactly what they are—scarred but refined, imperfect but beautiful. They are us.

Guests are invited to write about their fears, bind their writings into small scrolls, and bury their fears into the pockets that serve as tombs for our burdens, vaults for our secrets, or sepulchers in which to lay our pains to rest. The scrolls are enclosed in the wall that, like us, is dappled with scars. We graze our hands upon the threaded scars in acknowledgment of our distress among the many. Paralleling the spiritual and sometimes quiet exchange that occurs in compassion, there is also a hushed physical exchange that takes place with every touch—while the oils from our hands are unnoticeably absorbed by the cotton threads, our fingertips will lift the invisible salt crystals of the Pacific Ocean water with which these scars have been anointed.

sundown

for years she was the only one
i showed these poems to
i prefer it that way
no one reading us

to be born into love
is an awakening

for light is the organizing principle of matter

awakened she says by the feminine soul of Christ in the nucleus
of the Anima Christi even as splitting occurs by crushing the skin
between two solids and this is called laceration see hands
feet body skull orbital bones cheekbones jaw iliac crest perineum

fusion resurrects us so no art can make us abandon our daughters
no poetry o God can set them out upon the wilderness without
also walking us home hand in hand with them

vi.1

quiet holy a certain darkness desires chaos
knifings rope burns at the neck prostitution
then too there is the darkness that desires
your kiss most intimate o most intimate light
for this finally is the last dark
into which we altogether descend and from which we die

to be kissed again and after three nights kissed

the first day the terror comes she and i panic

at manzanar tule lake topaz and heart mountain
and the second day and every day thereafter we take courage
now we are prepared to die said endō and melanie rae now we are ready

the first day she and i are who we are
the second day we are who we were born to be
the third is her beautiful belief in life after life

vi.2

i have received
beatings
from men
so that my face
split open and
blood poured down my neck
like communion

thermonuclear bombs in abundance o creator o destroyer of worlds
with a fission avalanche fusion follows fusion
and the morphogenetic biophoton field equals
the development of the embryo

conversing with you my wife comes to me
like a swan descending she lies down
all our days one day all our nights nights opened by your hands

vi.3

finding hydrogen the most abundant element
on earth the sun's light makes hydrogen bombs
mobilizing outward force by nuclear fusion
with whole families laid waste from far distances
scalp contusions are still detected by mirror
through incisions from the aponeurotic surface

likewise my father picked fattened ticks from our old bird dog
and dropped them in a bucket of gasoline

they littered her body like garlic cloves like our own forgetfulness
too enamored with ourselves or too much ash in our eyes
we need you to love our nakedness and teach us to love again

our children
grew up meek or murderous
and we blamed you

vi.4

some say dying is not strange or hard
but a return to our mothers and fathers
who stood before mighty winds
from the beginning

you spoke light good light
in the great cities
our bodies shimmer
like silver on the edge of the earth
or lit blue by dusk over the badger two-medicine range
in northern montana where she and i die quickly with our sisters
and brothers five years before the 20th century closes Hanoi releases
the numbers 2 million civilians 1.5 million north south war dead

your graceful words accompanying us
o mercy bed and maiden death

vi.5

we found devotion in emptiness
she and i emptied into you

before thermonuclear impact light sound heat and air
are pulled back to the detonation point
and expelled again flattening the city

the body is atomic fission
stacking to harmonic fusion through abnormal bedlam
deuterium and trillium brought together
with subatomic violence
after we're dead we seek you
and early in the morning find you
the plain things of the world are yours
dogwood and cattail
scapula petal and plume

vi.6

we were never meant for lonely childhoods
opened from the late burn of nations
burning finally out

o God with your light we control fission and fracture but fusion
is too volatile too much to witness so much like the limestone reefs rising
over the rocky mountain front one reef thirteen miles long a thousand feet
high

surround us as we hold our chests
and breathe as we breathe your name

our figures are resurrections
the flesh absorbing and emanating light
like monseigneur myriel or the sublime Christ of critical theory
a single small wound can cause death from shock
and internal hemorrhaging
the imprint of when we were forsaken

vi.7

our prayers
do not create you in your image you create us
to be forsaken broken freed from the death drive
as yarrow roots ground themselves in you

prison and the death penalty are the legacy of slavery
and genocide rooted in subatomic unities annihilated going forth
to set the world on fire but love is asymmetry
creating life and certain annihilations
aligned with life *ite inflammate omnia*

to understand any society we must understand
the women and the men and what is between them

enthrall us in you wholly lost take us to you me to her her to me
as trees take to sky lifting
lead us where you want us to go

vi.8

against indifference and greed
to reach love whole skeins of quantum scientists
convert from cold dark to spectral light
after witnessing death by the maximum security school to prison pipeline

and though white space fear insists on itself
intimacy expands like goldenrod through space and time
with energies capable of pulverizing matter

but holy Christ what does Christ mean again
in critical theology perhaps everything we know
is that the dark places exist
supremely now the police brutality the killings
but surfacing cupped in his hand cupped to my face

to speak american psalms sonnets use color to penetrate the horror

and i am my beloved's and he is mine don't let go we need holding

vi.9

don't give up our sons either Lord
don't let us abandon them did you abandon your son
my God why have you forsaken us

he said

and we abandoned him

as you knew we would
from temporal to immortal matter
energy is matter multiplied multiple times
by the speed of light

at the light barrier he was forsaken
so we keep on under you God
o cut us from the cloth sew into us a little death
each death a part of the whole
darkness o never abandon us again

vi.10

with good brothers
we without vision without light inner or ocular
we who perish like the flower in the field wait for light

this one wronged
beaten by his own father whipped
but when he became a man he not only forgave his father
who had little in life and little opportunity
he bought him a house and placed his father on firm ground
the image of father and son embracing
weeping on each other's necks stays with me forever

you are a poet of reconciliation
i mean she and i see you as a poet
of blessing we who were homeless exiled sick with longing
you blessed us all

vi.11

From 1975 to 1979, my father-in-law, Phơủl Vân Thạch, a high-ranking official of the South Vietnamese Army, was imprisoned in one of the many re-education camps in Việt Nam. This photo was taken during his capture. Gaunt and marred, his gentle hands still carry the eminent strength that upholds his loyalty and his name. From 1979 to 1982, he and his family escaped on foot from Việt Nam, through Cambodia, and into Thailand, where they arrived at the refugee camp before stepping foot onto American soil.

I marvel at the profound love that ignited our predecessors with the courage to fight for a generation that did not yet exist. Bác Phơủl survived seventeen bullet wounds during the war. I have recreated these war wounds by rubbing rainwater and tears into the paper with my fingers as an anointing, expressing the immense gratitude for all he has done for our people, for our generation, and for those who will go on to inherit these freedoms. The words *Ba Ơi* are repeatedly hand-painted in Sanskrit as a heavy rain that pours upon our Fathers, and hearkens unto them.

> *For a seed to achieve its greatest expression, it must come completely undone. The shell cracks, its insides come out and everything changes. To someone who doesn't understand growth, it would look like complete destruction.*
> —Cynthia Occelli

Although these afflictions set out to maim, they've only broken open the fissures that have made space for seeds to nestle and for new growth to occur.

Blessed *is* the man who endures
... for when he has been
... the

night

even the dark is not dark
to you or the night-blooming
hypnotic-scented cereus

even night is as the day we first met

we sometimes encounter avulsion
grinding compression
by weight by steel wheels passing
over chest and limbs lead metal and glass
tearing the skin the margins irregular uneven

yet we were married in a single knowing
light quantum borne in electrons
at night networks of stars and a breath
her instep touched to my calf the arch of her
ribs your handiwork in my hands

vii.1

light is more contained less fractured
in healthy cells light are your kisses o God
light are the kisses of your mouth
harmonize us o marry us
to each other to the world and you

we drop fire bombs followed by atomic wounding
among the thousand-fold wounding from which we never recover

in your memory we are no longer at war here or overseas
the city a melody like mountain blue jays
over sylvan lake let him kiss me with the kisses she says
of his mouth for your love is wine

mystic and east rosebud in the beartooth range
where the absaroka wilderness sets the yellowstone
north to the missouri then south to the gulf of mexico

vii.2

we want to be done
with cutting and killing ourselves
we want to usher the beast into and out of our hearts
i believe we are all abandoned
all loved

immanuel means God with us and we burn like stars

crippled hydrogen atoms no longer absorb or emit light
but can be resurrected by choice

deep tissue unevenly divided
foreign bodies in the wound
a curved laceration made of rock or water
the skin torn free or undermined
blood is life that's why we carry small stones in our pockets
and set them in the vault of heaven

vii.3

cut edges are normally clean
length greater than width the wound usually
spindle shaped leaving more blood on the long plain before the great
mountains
where the genocided women walk with lanterns alongside those who
delivered genocide
women and men loved whole in the house made of dawn

your miracles reside in montana and in the bedroom where momaday
sleeps

every day i see my cousin jacine and my brother and me holding hands
over the river the summer before she died jacine wore the shirt of flame
so did charlie calf robe paul deputy and bobby jones who hung himself
while the other three were shot or bludgeoned to death and i said we all
wear
the shirt of flame and my teacher said some more than others some so
much more
how is it i was deeply loved by them i still don't know
the motherless empty the fatherless hungry dismay so dark in my jawbone
o God that's why i cry into the wooden bowl of my hands

vii.4

clubbing instruments cause skull fractures fissured depressed comminuted
the skull inbuckled the bones broken in several places
near here is the town where children were gassed to death or burned in
industrial ovens
human bodies burn readily the hands and feet drop off under sudden
intense heat
all men young and old in broad daylight three bullets each head chest
chest murder

in the house of dawn which is your house
on a long hill outside prague hidden in roses
symphonic atoms rosettes of nuclear light in the wrist bones of those dead
in the garden

of friendship and peace in the shadows where the children of my grand-
mother's massacred ones
hold hands with the children of those who massacred them
my children of peace with me my children of war planting
a hundred thousand roses again o wounds of God with us always
my God Christ where is my wife where are my children

                                        vii.5

dear God our nameless one
we love our daughters and sons
but do not let us forsake our fathers

o name above all names
let us love them with electromagnetic gravitational force
for forsaking them we forsake ourselves each father understood
as the dynamics of a field the cut is deeper at entry due to greater pressure
the head leads to the tailing a blade entered obliquely bevels one edge
at the other's expense for atomic life absorbs light
but a horizontal blade causes a flap wound

o let us love them

Lord let us go to them with joy in our eyes
preparing them for death by asking forgiveness and by forgiving them
their tritium boosting their double yield so they can die knowing

vii.6

you sense us she and i brought to blossom

with you we don't live by ourselves
and we don't die alone either

beauty like smoke through the doorway
of worlds beyond division we die with each
other and happily the images we make of you are nothing
compared to the bodies you give us
light waves loops and strings light bullets
portable never-ending o numinous *mysterium tremendum*
et fascinans et flame the ultimate danger
fear-invoking fear-transcending merciful compassionate
your touch the press of my hand to her forehead and hips
the zenith of her ribs her curved bones set over
the opening you made for the infinite

                                        vii.7

in the beginning
a burden of water a veil of light
the word was a cyclone at the edge of the eye

a chop wound a blow with the cutting end of a heavy instrument
an axe a butcher knife a machete a sword
the margins sharp and deep john the son of thunder said the weak inter-
action
is radioactive decay is essential the word was love was light was God
essential nuclear fission and fusion with God all things came into being

apart from God nothing came into being

the word a continuous range of electromagnetic gravitational energy

heat color light of the snail's nautilus
o crown rack of bull elk
the neckline the life cluster and edible thistle
blue iris foxteeth boxwood and blue-eyed grass

vii.8

our mothers are your mother
with sacred heart ablaze
and my father as he moves through ancient mountains

fir and lodgepole above clear rivers below black skies

you the storm we flee the storm we return to
rainsoaked running the gorge
at pine creek in the beartooth wilderness where lightning rings
from canyon walls and our mouths eat fire

the magnitude of your love still frightens us

i've met too many old pale men who say Christ
is with them but treat their mothers ugly
their wives and daughters and other women along with their country

the velocity of light is 186,000 miles per second

the gravitational force attracts anything with mass

vii.9

but blessed are those who listen
to the poverty of wildflowers
and find night so near dawn

over a dismembered animal
bears still remember the bugle bloom
about to shout and how penetrating
wounds puncture the body cavity

tissue and muscle
sinew and joints and bone

but unlike bears we forget how the night shines
we go about forgetting the force manifest
in electric fields magnetic fields
and light marsh hollyhock buttonweed redstem storksbill
fated by need we hastily imprint violence

vii.10

in the darkness she and i thank you
and we listen to each other so now that we're older
she still presses her face to mine
and i still lay my head on her chest asking her as we die
where are you going hearing her say i'm going to God

where what is least familiar is most named
and what is most sublime is least comprehended

at night i cup my hand to the back of her head the line of her jaw
our worldskin a dark conflation of night and light
so when she looks into me i see you
the body the city trillium deer's-head orchid fawn lily

with my name hidden she draws herself over me
and kisses me and we both soon slumber

your beauty our night all light

vii.11

129

Hồn Mình Hơn Mình, 2012. Hand embroidery and oil on canvas. 48 x 48 inches.

Since antiquity, the laurel wreath has been donned as a symbol of triumph. Exhausted from all that he has had to endure, a man is crowned by Grace. With his eyes ever set upon victory, he abides in the unyielding Faith that has delivered him from wars past and wars to come.

The hand stitching reads, *"Hồn mình hơn mình"*, a Vietnamese phrase that translates to *"Our spirit is greater than us."* Breathing in as I puncture the canvas and breathing out as I pull the thread, this physical rhythm assists me in meditating upon the power that can be found in the Spirit.

To all who have fallen short of breath during Life's battles: Let us cultivate the Will to overcome these adversities that indeed refine us. We shall triumph.

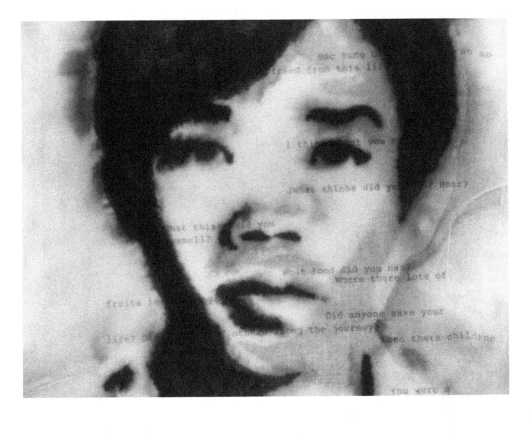

Bác Hùng and *Sisters* (*In the Spirit of Humanitarianism for the Refugee People*), 2015.
From the *Quiet* installation.

The creation of this piece called for the quiet spaces in which I worked in reverence of lives lost. I contemplated the quiet that came before the storm that funneled so tightly around our people. The quiet in which they walked, treading upon dead leaves and the detritus of life around them. The voices that were made to quiet in the jungles while hiding from enemy forces. The quiet in which they prayed to their God and looked to their ancestors, as they pled for their lives and the lives of those they loved. This quiet that heavily drapes over us when we gather to mourn the departed. The quiet in which prayer flags billow.

One of the traditional Vietnamese funerary rituals is for family members to don white sashes upon their heads to signify their relationship to the departed. I have recreated these mourning bands to honor the lives of our mothers and fathers, sisters and brothers, aunts and uncles, daughters and sons, whom we lost during the war. This piece was originally inspired by a collection of letters that I discovered in the Southeast Asian Archive, letters that were written by family members, pleading for help to find their loved ones who went missing during the escape. Each portrait is raised in respect for those who did not survive to see new shores. Using the typewriter that I inherited from Cô Bé, my youngest auntie, I retyped these letters upon each sash, weaving the words of their family members with my own words to them.

This piece is dedicated to the courageous individuals who risked their lives for the freedom into which I was born.

acknowledgments
and dedications

with gratitude to editors Kristin George Bagdanov, Joe Hoover, Robert Nazarene, Patty Paine, Susan Sink, and William Slaughter (Mudlark featured 33 poems in the chapbook atomic theory 432) who first published these poems, sometimes in different forms:

"early dark" in The American Journal of Poetry

"i.1"	the body is the city
"i.2"	you witnessed you walked—for Hiền and Trinh Mai Thạch
"i.3"	bless the harm we do
"i.4"	the city is black
"i.5"	everything held together—for Adrienne Rich and Thomas Sleigh
"i.6"	you didn't abandon us—for Pierre Teilhard de Chardin
"i.7"	fatherless fathers
"i.8"	even in darkness
"i.9"	she and i love you
"i.10"	out of the black body

"before dawn" in Mudlark

"ii.1"	century man teeth haggard
"ii.2"	o hold us in your arms—for Madelaine L'Engle and Li-Young Lee
"ii.3"	and so she believes
"ii.4"	once
"ii.5"	on the mountain—for Teresa of Avila
"ii.6"	we want to ask your forgiveness—for Leslie Marmon Silko

"ii.7"   in the capital city
"ii.8"   beaten taken
"ii.9"   where bear claws
"ii.10"   those better than me
"ii.11"   she and i often say

"sunrise" in Mudlark
"iii.1"   these fatherless fathers
"iii.2"   here in the still point
"iii.3"   we have tongues—for Martin Luther King, Jr.
"iii.4"   on the third day
"iii.5"   we abandoned our children
"iii.6"   the planets exist—for Simone Weil
"iii.7"   at sunrise made of night
"iii.8"   the stars are not lonely
"iii.9"   we have a mother
"iii.10"   i've used a bone saw—for Hannah Arendt
"iii.11"   o God creating

"midday" in Mudlark
"iv.1"   she kisses me
"iv.2"   my wife wants us to know—for Yusef Komunyakaa
"iv.3"   we are alive—for bell hooks
"iv.4"   she places her body
"iv.5"   we hear—for Makoto Fujimura and Eliza Griswold
"iv.6"   you are—for Corretta Scott King and Claudia Rankine
"iv.7"   we need you—for Lucille Clifton and Sherman Alexie
"iv.8"   the smell of smoke—for Kateřina Rudčenková and Anton
          Wildgans
"iv.9"   in this world
"iv.10"   world without—for Shūsaku Endō and Anna Akhmatova
"iv.11"   everything has always existed

"sundown" in Diode
"v.1"   in late light—for Nâzım Hikmet
"v.2"   we don't need to act like we don't see you—for Tomáš Halík
"v.3"   she and i—for Layli Long Soldier
"v.4"   my wife whispers—for John Rutter
"v.5"   sorrow of the great sorrow—for Fred Moten

"v.6"   i was born in the city of industry
"v.7"   o make us—for Carolyn Forché, Emmanuel Levinas, and
           Martin Buber
"v.8"   we too like schwarzchild's dark stars
"v.9"   she and i walked with you God—for Toni Morrison
"v.10"   when i was a boy
"v.11"   two things dostoyevsky said

"dusk" in Ruminate
     "vi.1"   for years
     "vi.2"   quiet holy
     "vi.3"   i have received
     "vi.4"   finding hydrogen
     "vi.5"   some say dying
     "vi.6"   we found devotion—for C.D. Wright
     "vi.7"   we were—for Victor Hugo, Michel Foucault, and Jacques
                 Derrida
     "vi.8"   our prayers—for Angela Davis and Judith Butler
     "vi.9"   against indifference—for Jericho Brown and Maggie Smith
     "vi.10"   don't give up—for William Blake

"dusk" in America
     "vi.11"   with good brothers; or bona annuntiatio

"night" in Bearings
     "vii.1"   even the dark
     "vii.2"   light is more
     "vii.3"   we want
     "vii.4"   cut edges
     "vii.5"   clubbing instruments—for Marie Uchytilová
     "vii.6"   dear God
     "vii.7"   you sense us—for Rudolf Otto
     "vii.8"   in the beginning
     "vii.9"   our mothers
     "vii.10"   but blessed are those—for Louise Erdrich and Mary Oliver
     "vii.11"   in the darkness

Shann Ray's work has been featured in Poetry, Esquire, McSweeney's, Poetry International, Narrative, Prairie Schooner, and Salon. He spent part of his childhood on the Northern Cheyenne reservation in southeast Montana and has served as a scholar of leadership and forgiveness studies in Africa, Asia, Europe, and the Americas. He is the author of *Sweetclover*, *Blood Fire Vapor Smoke*, *American Masculine*, *Balefire*, and *Forgiveness and Power in the Age of Atrocity*. He lives with his wife and daughters in Spokane, Washington, and teaches at Gonzaga University.